The Fourth Estate

Journalism in North America

The African American Press

Derek Miller

Cavendish Square

New York

Published in 2019 by Cavendish Square Publishing, LLC
243 5th Avenue, Suite 136, New York, NY 10016

Copyright © 2019 by Cavendish Square Publishing, LLC

First Edition

Library of Congress Cataloging-in-Publication Data

Names: Miller, Derek L., author.
Title: The African American press / Derek Miller.
Description: First edition. | New York : Cavendish Square, 2019. |
Series:The fourth estate | Includes bibliographical references and index.
Identifiers: LCCN 2017060408 (print) | LCCN 2018000092 (ebook) |
ISBN 9781502634801 (eBook) | ISBN 9781502634795 (library bound) |
ISBN 9781502634818 (pbk.) | ISBN 9781502634825 (6 pack)
Subjects: LCSH: African American press--History--Juvenile literature. |
African Americans--Civil rights--Juvenile literature. |
United States--Race relations--History--Juvenile literature.
Classification: LCC PN4882.5 (ebook) | LCC PN4882.5 .M54 2019 (print) |
DDC 071.308996073--dc23
LC record available at https://lccn.loc.gov/2017060408

Editorial Director: David McNamara
Editor: Caitlyn Miller
Copy Editor: Nathan Heidelberger
Associate Art Director: Amy Greenan
Designer: Lindsey Auten
Production Coordinator: Karol Szymczuk
Photo Research: J8 Media

Printed in the United States of America

CONTENTS

The Fourth Estate

Journalism in North America

FREEDOM'S JOURNAL.

"RIGHTEOUSNESS EXALTETH A NATION."

CORNISH & RUSSWURM, *Editors and Proprietors.*

NEW-YORK, FRIDAY, MAY 18, 1827.

VOL. I. N

TOUSSAINT L'OUVERTURE.

(Concluded.)

Such was the man to whom the island was ndebted for its prosperity: which, however, vas unfortunately not of long continuance.—No sooner was the peace of Amiens definitively settled, than Buonaparte, determined on the recovery of the colony, the reinstatement of the former proprietors, and the subugation of the emancipated slaves.

On the arrival in the bay of Samana of the French fleet, having on board twenty-five housand men, the flower of the French army, nder the command of General Le Clerc, the rother-in-law of Buonaparte, Toussaint hastened to the spot to reconnoitre its movements. Having never before seen so numerous a fleet, 'We shall all perish,' said he, to is officers; all France is come to St. Domingo." The division under Rochambeau having ffected a landing at Fort Dauphin, the neroes who had assembled in crowds to behold he strange sight, were charged with the baynet, and numbers of them killed on the spot; ut the main body of the fleet and army, on reparing to land at Cape Francois, received message from General Christophe, prohibiory of any disembarkation of troops without he orders of his commander in chief. Le Clerc, on this, sent a letter to Christophe, with mingled expressions of conciliation and menace, to which Christophe replied, with reat firmness and moderation, that he was esponsible for his conduct only to the govrnor and commander-in-chief, Toussaint L'Ouverture; that if he attempted to carry his hreats into execution, he should know how o resist as became a general officer; and hat he accounted those troops which he hreatened to land as so many pieces of card, which the slightest breath of wind would issipate. Le Clerc had sent on shore printd copies of a proclamation drawn up by Buonaparte, in which the same insidious mixture of cajoling and the threatening was sed to seduce or intimidate the blacks. 'Inhabitants of St. Domingo,' it commenced, 'whatever be your origin or your colour, you re all French: you are all free, and all equal efore God, and before the republic;' and it oncluded, 'Rally round the captain-general: he brings you peace and plenty. Whoever shall dare to separate himself from him vill be a traitor to his country, and the indignation of the republic will devour him as the re devours your dried canes.

This menace, backed by such an overwhelming force, shook the allegiance of the white inhabitants to Toussaint; Christophe erceived the disaffection, and knowing the own not to be defensible, set fire to it in several places, retreating in good order, and arrying off with him above two thousand of he whites as hostages not one of whom was njured, in the confusion and massacres which ollowed. This spirited measure, and the active preparations making by Toussaint in the nterior, induced Le Clerc to make trial of a cheme, which, if resorted to previous to the ommencement of hostilities, might hav een successful. He had brought out with im the two sons of Toussaint, whom the fa her was to be permitted to see, in the hope hat, through them, he might be prevailed pon to acquiesce in the wishes of the First Consul. From the smoking ruins of Cape Francois, Coisnon, their tutor, was despatched with his pupils, to Toussaint's dence. The interview was he artful pedagogue employ uence to prevail on Toussain he chief command, and becor ant-general of Le Clerc; but Toussaint had made his arrangements to oppose the French army, and, after an interview of two hours, left his two sons to decide between their father and their adopted country. In the *History* it is stated that the sons returned to General Le Clerc, and were never heard of more; but Lacroix says, that the mother succeeded in detaining them, and that one of them was afterwards intrusted with the command of a body of insurgents.

When Le Clerc found that Toussaint was inexorable, he issued a proclamation, declaring the generals Toussaint and Christophe to be put out of the protection of the law, and ordering every citizen to pursue and treat them as rebels to the French republic. The

which he was but too successful. The black generals La Plume and Maurepas, went over with their forces to the French: and what was their recompense? Lacroix confirms, to the letter what King Henry has stated in his able manifesto of September, 1814:

'Maurepas, a man of mild and gentle manners, esteemed by his fellow citizens for his integrity, had been one of the first to join the French, and had rendered them the most signal services; yet this man was suddenly carried off to port de Paix, and put on board the Admiral's vessels, then at anchor in the roads, where, after binding him to the mainmast, they, in derision, with nails, such as are used in ship building, fixed two old epaulets on his shoulders, and an old general's hat on his head. In that frightful condition, these cannibals, after having glutted their savage mirth, precipitated him, with his wife and children into the sea! Such was the fate of this virtuous, and unfortunate soldier!'

Toussaint, however, had under his immediate command, a well disciplined army; and Dessalines, one of the most courageous, enterprising and skilful of all the negro generals held the strong fortress of Crete pierrot, which had been built by the English. The French army laid seige to this place, which after a brave defence, was evacuated by Dessalines, who carried off every thing that was valuable, leaving a small detachment to follow him in the morning. Intoxicated with the successful issue of the siege, the French committed all manner of cruelties on the unfortunate negroes who fell into their hands; and Le Clerc, with equal baseness and folly, publicly restored to the proprietors of estates all their ancient authority. The consequence was such as might have been foreseen; all the blacks who had adhered to the French now deserted them, and again took up arms, Le Clerc perceived his error, and had once more resource to the delusion of proclaiming 'liberty and equality to all the inhabitants of St. Domingo, without regard to colour;' with the reservation, however, of the approval of the French government.—The negroes, tired of the war, again deserted their leaders; and at length, Christophe negotiated in behalf of himself, his colleague Dessalines, and Toussaint the general in chief, a general amnesty for all their troops, and the preservation of the respective ranks of all the black officers. Le Clerc was too happy to grant these conditions; and a peace was accordingly concluded, by which the sovereignty of France over the Island of St. Domingo was acknowledged by all the constituted authorities.

Toussaint had liberty to retire to any of his estates which he might please to make choice of. He selected that called by his own name, L'Ouverture, situated at Gonaives; there, in the bosom of his family, he entered upon the enjoyment of that repose of which he had so long been deprived. The secret instructions however of Buonaparte were now to be obeyed: and Le Clerc lost no time in putting into execution an act which has entitled everlasting disgrace on his memory. In the dead of night, a ship of the line and a frigate anchored near Gonaives, and landed a body of troops; they surrounded the house of Toussaint, when Brunet, a brigadier-general, entered the chamber where he slept, with a

were taken, and Le Clerc ordered them to be shot. He then caused about one hundred of the confidential friends of Toussaint to be arrested, and sent to the different ships of the squadron; none of them were ever heard of afterwards, and it is supposed that they were thrown overboard.

Toussaint on the passage was kept a close prisoner, and separated from his wife and family; and on the arrival of the ship at Brest, he was merely allowed to see them once and take leave of them for ever. He was conducted to the castle of Joux in Normandy, with a single negro to attend on him; his wife and children were conveyed to Bayonne, and nothing more was ever heard of either. On

which became, as doubtless was intended, his sepulchre;—the floor being actually covered with water. Thus did this great and good man perish.

—ooo—

From the Abolition Intelligencer.

The surprising influence of prejudice.

That savage nations enveloped in the darkness of ignorance, inured to scenes of rapine and cruelty and murder, should become so lost to all the finer sensibilities of our nature as that "their tender mercies are cruel," is not a matter of very great astonishment. But it is really something more than marvellous that the man whose character has been humanized by civilization, whose mind has been illumined by the rays of science, and whose heart has been renovated by the power of the gospel, should become the advocate of the cruel policy of those dark and ruthless sons of nature.

Should the origin of African slavery be enquired for, it must be sought among the most barbarous nations, and will be found growing out of the most sordid and malignant passions of the human heart; while fraud and violence have in almost every instance, been the means by which our slaves were originally procured. Yet are there multitudes in our own enlightened country, in our boasted land of liberty, who, with the book of God in their hands, and a public profession of allegiance to the compassionate Saviour in their mouths, unblushingly stand forth as the advocates of this cruel system.

How shall we account for such conduct? By supposing hat such characters are sturdy hypocrites, who have continued to do violence to their own sense of duty until "their consciences have become seared as with a hot iron?" This may in some instances be the fact; but we are persuaded that in most cases their conduct should be regarded merely as a specimen of the surprising influence of prejudice on the human mind. The prejudices of education, of example, and self interest, all uniting, prepare the mind to receive the most glaring sophistry and to settle down upon its deductions as securely as upon those of the most logical reasoning.

In our last we attended to the argument drawn from the colour of our slaves in support of African slavery. In the present No. we will notice that which is drawn from the *assumed* fact of the inferiority of the blacks in point of intellect. That the blacks are inferior to the whites in intellectual powers is constantly asserted with the utmost confidence as a fact by the advocates of the system. And from this fact they seem to think the inference fair that they were intended for slaves. But we do not hesitate to declare that the fact is gratuitously assumed, and that the history of mankind not only contradicts but abundantly refutes the assumption.

But before we refer to history we ask how is this inferiority of African intellect to be established? By comparing the slave with his master? Yes, the poor African born in the land of strangers, denied the advantages of education, excluded from all means of mental improvement, bowed down under the burden of a hopeless and perpetual slavery, without any motive to exertion, save the fear of the lash, is brought into contrast with the high minded and aspiring son of fortune, ho has been dandled on the lap of affluence, voured with all the advantages of education, and stimulated with the high hopes of istinguishing his character, immortalizing is name, and ennobling his posterity. Is his fair, is it candid, is it honest?

And almost equally unfair would it be to compare the inhabitants of our own country, or of any of the civilized nations of Europe, with the barbarous and uncivilized tribes of Africa; and from the comparison to pronounce an original and permanent inferiority of mind as characterising the African. Let it be remembered that climate and manners and customs and religion and government all have influence in giving character to a nation, and that in all these respects the African labours under an obvious disadvantage. Nevertheless their character is doubtless far superior to what is generally represented by those who feel interested in defaming them.

Now keeping in mind the
tages under which for so m
have laboured both at home
us turn our attention to the
few individuals whom histor
having, by the energies of
geniuses, arisen to a degre
which not only rescues thei
charge of original inferiori
also sheds a brilliancy and d
own characters.

Hannibal, an African w
ved a good education, ros
lieutenant-general and dire
under Peter the great of R
ginning of the last century.

The son of Hannibal, abo
mulatto, was lieutenant-gen
sian corps of artillery. *Gre*

Francis Williams, a black,
maica about the close of the
He was sent to England an
the University of Cambridge
turn to Jamaica he opene
taught Latin and the mathem
many pieces in Latin verse
covered, considerable talen
219.

Antony Williams Amo was
and brought to Europe wher
Under the patronage of
Brunswick, he pursued his
in Saxony, and at Wittem
greatly distinguished himse
and good conduct. In 1734
gree of doctor in philosophy
ty of Wittemberg." "Skill
edge of the Greek and La
and "having examined the
cients and moderns," he de
lectures on philosophy" wi
ance. "In 1744 he suppo
Wittemberg, and published
on the absence of sensation
its presence in the human
"appointed professor," and
supported a thesis "on the
ought to be made between t
mind and those of sense."
commends these "two di
evincive of a mind "exercis
and addicted to "abstruse d
the opinion of Blumenbach
much well digested knowle
physiological works of the t
moir of Amo, "published at
academic council, his integ
dustry, and erudition, are
mended." Gregoire was un
what became of him after
173—176. *Rees under man.*

Job. Ben Solomon, son of
king of Banda, on the Gamb
1730 and sold in Maryland.
found his way to England, w
dignified air, and amenity c
cured him friends, among th
Sloane, for whom he transla
bic manuscripts. After bei
di tinction at the Court of S
sent back to Bunda. The
afterwards wrote to his fri
and America were publish
with interest. This man is
able to repeat the koran from
p. 160—161.

James Eliza John Capitein
rica. At the age of eight h
on the river St. Andre by a
made a present of him to o
By the latter he was car
where he employed himself
acquired the elements of th
Hebrew, and Chaldaic lan
terwards went to the Unive
where he devoted himself
theology. "Having studie
took his degrees, and in 17
Calvinistic minister to Gui
came of him was never k
Holland he published an ele
two Latin dissertations, (on
of the Gentiles, and the o
and a small volume of se
196—207.

coast of Africa, "is very supe
capacity to the generality of
America. They are more so

Freedom's Journal, the first newspaper of the African American press, began in 1827.

Slavery and the Abolitionist Movement

At the beginning of the 1800s, the plight of African Americans in the United States was quite grave. In the South, the institution of slavery was unchallenged. At the turn of the century, nearly a million slaves labored in appalling conditions. By the time the Emancipation Proclamation declared an end to slavery in 1863, that number had grown to four million. Meanwhile, in the North, free African Americans were not seen as equal citizens. Newspapers stereotyped and ridiculed them. White abolitionists—who campaigned for an end to slavery—often portrayed blacks as childlike and simple people who needed help from whites. Favorable portrayals of African Americans were nearly impossible to find, and this was not only a problem in the press of the time. The attitudes of ordinary Americans toward blacks were generally quite racist and prejudiced.

On March 16, 1827, African Americans began to push back against these stereotypes in print. *Freedom's Journal,* the country's first newspaper owned and operated by African Americans, was founded in New York City. It published rebuttals to the racist tirades that filled the many white-owned newspapers of the day. Positive stories about African Americans were also included in its pages, as well as a record of the horrible violence that African Americans were subject to at the time. Lynchings and other instances of racial violence would often go unreported in the white press.

Freedom's Journal was short-lived, but it sparked a new era in the United States. African Americans began to set up newspapers across the country. White abolitionists were no longer the primary voice advocating for an end to slavery in print. Free African Americans across the North advocated for an end to slavery, as well as for more favorable treatment for free blacks in the United States.

When slavery finally did end more than thirty years later, the African American press turned its attention to other matters. Ending segregation, the unequal treatment of blacks and whites, and securing the right to vote for all African Americans became their focus. They also looked unflinchingly at the horrifying racial violence of the period.

African Americans in the North and South were subject to lynchings and race riots. Lynchings were often treated as festive events, when black people were chased and murdered in grisly ways by white mobs in their Sunday best. These mobs served to intimidate African Americans communities or punish alleged "crimes" by African Americans, such as refusing to offer the respect to which whites felt they were entitled. Likewise, so-called race riots were frequently acts of mob violence carried out by whites against black people. Sometimes, the black populations of entire cities were forced to flee as police looked on without interfering in the communal violence.

This book will focus primarily on the African American press from the time of *Freedom's Journal* to the end of the civil rights era of the 1950s and 1960s. With the end of the civil rights era, most blatant civil rights abuses came to an end in the United States. Further attempts to limit the right to vote and segregate African Americans would become much less direct. The era of government-supported segregation had come to an end. However, the African American press continues. It remains a moral compass for the country, pointing out injustice and demanding equal treatment for all people.

The White Press

Prior to the year 1827 and the founding of *Freedom's Journal*, African Americans were almost universally portrayed in a negative light in the press. Unsurprisingly, their most favorable treatment was by the abolitionists. Abolitionism was a movement that sought to end slavery. It had many prominent members—especially in the North. Abolitionists published newspapers that defended their views and criticized the institution of slavery. Most prominent abolitionists were white, and prior to the Civil War they were the most vocal supporters of African Americans.

However, abolitionists were not without their flaws. The views expressed in their newspapers tended to contain the racism and prejudices of the time. Although they favored the end of slavery, many did not truly believe blacks were equal to whites. Furthermore, they often did not want to draw attention to the racism and prejudice that free African Americans experienced in the North. Their primary concern was only the abolition of slavery in the South.

Furthermore, the Northern press outside of the abolitionists was even more fiercely critical of African Americans. Writers typically portrayed black people as hopelessly inferior to whites. The racism of the time was explicit and contemptuous in leading newspapers around the country.

One important newspaper editor of the time was Mordecai Noah. He gave voice to the views that many white New Yorkers held in numerous articles published during the early nineteenth century:

> The fifteenth part of the population of this city is composed of blacks. Only fifteen are qualified to vote. Freedom is a great blessing, indeed, to them. They swell our list of paupers, they are indolent, and uncivil. And yet if a black man commits a crime, we have more interest made for him than for a white.

Noah's influence was such that it led historians to the "Noah thesis"—the idea that *Freedom's Journal* was founded specifically to combat the racist views espoused by Noah. However, this view has fallen out of favor recently, given the fact that Noah's prejudiced views were not uncommon for the time.

As you might expect, newspapers in the South were even less sympathetic toward African Americans than those in the North. Their pages were filled with the mundane and disturbing articles that underpinned the institution of slavery: ads for selling and buying human beings, as well as rewards for the return of fugitive slaves to their masters.

Southern newspapers also actively defended the institution of slavery. One column published in Virginia's *Staunton Spectator* on November 29, 1859, is representative of such views. It states that the "institution of slavery is ordained in Heaven, and ... the slaveholder who trusts in the Almighty arm will find that arm a refuge and a fortress." The author contends that slaves are in fact more fortunate than free blacks in the North: "We have never entertained a doubt that the condition of the Southern slaves is the best and most desirable for the negroes, as a class, that they have ever been found in or are capable of. There is abundant evidence to prove that the black man's lot as a slave, is vastly preferable to that of his free brethren at the North."

Unsurprisingly, the author feels the need to defend this view which is obviously false and indefensible. He does so by recounting a story of an escaped slave who yearns to return to his plantation in the South. He concludes this "is not an isolated case, but the experience of a large majority of emancipated slaves and run-away negroes in the Northern States." Needless to say, there was no widespread migration south into slavery as his article implies.

The Abolitionists and William Lloyd Garrison

Abolitionism was the movement to end the enslavement of black people in the United States and Europe. While slavery did not become widespread on the European continent, countries like Great Britain did engage in the slave trade around the world. Abolitionists across Europe eventually campaigned for an end to these practices.

From very early in American history, abolitionists were active in the country. Quakers—members of a branch of Christianity—were some of the most outspoken abolitionists beginning in the 1600s. However, abolitionists were not limited to any one religion or political party. They were united by their feeling that slavery was a terrible moral wrong and ought to be ended.

William Lloyd Garrison was one of the most famous and outspoken white abolitionists. He was considered to be rather radical during his time because of his demand for immediate emancipation for all slaves. Some other abolitionists were only willing to campaign for gradual emancipation.

Garrison worked for an abolitionist newspaper with Quaker roots before beginning his own newspaper, the *Liberator*, in 1831. Until the end of slavery more than thirty years later, Garrison railed against the institution of slavery in his paper. He also worked with prominent African American abolitionists to support the cause.

Abolitionist newspapers owned by whites set the stage for the flowering of the African American press that came after them. While their white allies made some progress, African Americans wanted to have a platform of their own to make their views known across the country and the world. The founding of *Freedom's Journal* and the newspapers that followed it made this possible.

William Lloyd Garrison campaigned for an end to slavery and for women to receive the right to vote.

Samuel E. Cornish was a pastor and editor of *Freedom's Journal*.

Freedom's Journal

To combat the stereotypes and racism of the press, a group of free African Americans in New York City founded *Freedom's Journal* in 1827. It was edited by two African American men: Samuel E. Cornish and John B. Russwurm. They published articles that promoted civil rights and denounced slavery, in addition to typical newspaper articles such as birth announcements and obituaries.

In its first issue, the two editors outlined their purpose for publishing the paper. They wanted to create a platform where African Americans could express their own views, rather than be represented by white abolitionists. They also wanted to combat the negative perceptions of black people that white newspapers were quick to reinforce.

Freedom's Journal never circulated in large numbers. Scholars estimate that less than a thousand copies were sold each week. However, its reach and impact were momentous. Copies of it were read not just by free blacks in the North but by slaves in the South. The stories and opinions of African Americans were no longer censored by white editors, who often shied away from pointing out racism and injustice.

After *Freedom's Journal* stopped publishing in 1829, other newspapers owned by African Americans sprang up to replace it. Over the years, their reach and influence grew. By the beginning of the Civil War in 1861, there were more than forty newspapers in print owned and operated by African Americans. Prejudiced white newspapers no longer had a monopoly on the spread of information.

This depiction of slaves picking cotton dates to the late 1800s.

A History of Subjugation

It is impossible to understand the importance of the African American press without looking at the long, violent history of oppression in the United States. Beginning with slavery and continuing through much of the twentieth century, African Americans suffered through centuries of persecution and mistreatment. They were denied basic human rights by the government, courts, and many of their fellow citizens who supported the climate of violent oppression that existed throughout much of the country.

1619–1865: Slavery in North America

Slavery took root in North America before the United States was a country. In 1619, approximately twenty enslaved Africans were brought to the British colony of Jamestown, Virginia. They were expected to do the difficult, backbreaking

John Brown's Raid in the Press

John Brown's raid on the United States arsenal at Harpers Ferry in 1859 is a seminal moment in American history. It is often credited as one of the major causes of the Civil War, which began just two years later. John Brown led a group of black and white abolitionists to attack the weapons store in the South. He hoped that slaves from the area would then rush to his aid, take up arms, and free even more slaves by force. However, the raid was a disaster and quickly failed. Many of Brown's men were killed, and the ones who were captured were hanged, including Brown himself.

Newspapers around the country labeled Brown a madman and a murderer—bystanders and

John Brown and his men were soon trapped in a besieged fire station with their hostages.

soldiers defending the arsenal had been killed during the raid. However, some Northern and abolitionist newspapers soon broke from this narrative. Most did not condone his violence but expressed sympathy for the ideal that drove Brown: an intense hatred of slavery. Brown's portrayal in the African American press was largely sympathetic. The African American press, too, did not focus on the violent reality of the raid. Instead, they lionized Brown the man. For example, the *Weekly Anglo African* called him a "martyr" and "redeemer."

Meanwhile, newspapers throughout the South denounced Brown's portrayal in the North. They began reporting as though further raids by armed abolitionists could be expected at any time. The rhetoric on both sides had reached a feverish pitch by December 1860, when South Carolina left the Union. Other Southern states followed in the coming months, and the bloody American Civil War began.

labor of cultivating tobacco on plantations. Alternative sources of cheap labor, like enslaved Native Americans and indentured servants—who performed free labor for a period before gaining their freedom—had proved less lucrative. The Native American slaves were susceptible to European diseases and died in large numbers. Indentured servants, most of whom were European, were much more expensive than slaves since they demanded better treatment than slaves and earned their freedom after a set number of years.

Enslaved Africans were considered property for life. All of their descendants were also born into slavery. Nevertheless, individual slave owners sometimes freed their slaves. Often, this happened when their owner died and the slaves' manumission was part of the owner's will. As a result, there was a sizeable population of free African Americans in the thirteen colonies—and later in the United States. Even in the South, free blacks lived in the same towns and cities as black slaves.

During this early period in American history, the institution of slavery put down much deeper roots in the South than in the North. Historians still debate the exact reason for this. There were likely economic reasons, such as slavery being more profitable for farmers in the South, as well as a difference in opinions between colonists in the North and South regarding the morality of the institution. Yet there were slaves in every Northern state throughout early American history. In some Northern states, slavery even continued up until the Civil War.

The treatment of slaves varied widely. Some masters were relatively kind to their slaves, while others were cruel and extremely violent. Many slaves were whipped and beaten by their owners. Even those slaves that were treated well had difficult lives that are hard to imagine. They were frequently separated from their spouses and children—often never to see them again. They could not marry or do ordinary activities like visit a neighboring town without the permission of their master. Additionally, the scarring experience of being sold for a price is one that many former slaves recounted with horror.

Before the founding of *Freedom's Journal* in 1827, there were few outlets for the views of African Americans. Not a single newspaper in the country was owned and operated by African Americans. However, some blacks in both the United States and European colonies of the Americas did publish books or pamphlets about their time as slaves. These slave narratives sometimes achieved popularity and were widely read in Europe

Reconstruction lasted from 1865 to 1877.

and the Americas by a white audience. They were often religious in their tone, with some focusing on a slave's conversion to Christianity after being brought from Africa to the New World.

1865–1968: Reconstruction, Jim Crow, and Segregation

After the end of the Civil War in 1865, slavery ended in the United States. However, the struggle for equal rights had just begun and would last for more than a century. Southern states were occupied by Union troops after the war, and African Americans were given the right to vote with the passing of the Fifteenth Amendment in 1870. Between 1863 and 1877, the Reconstruction Era took place. Southern states were forced to extend civil rights to blacks. African Americans were allowed to vote, and some Southern states even sent black congressmen to Washington, DC. But federal troops gradually pulled out of the South, and the states set up a system of racist laws popularly known as Jim Crow.

African Americans were prevented from voting through various means, such as poll taxes and literacy tests. The laws were written in such a way that former slaves had no hope of voting, while poor, uneducated whites were allowed to vote. The federal government turned a blind eye, and the courts did not strike down the racist laws. A system of racial segregation took shape across the South—and parts of the North. Blacks and whites had different schools, hospitals, and businesses. While they were supposed to be of equal quality, in practice, black public services were far worse. Poor schooling and health care prevented African Americans across the country from prospering.

Racial violence also flourished during this period. African Americans were harassed and intimidated by white mobs. Lynchings were a part of ordinary life for blacks throughout the country. White mobs murdered blacks with impunity; no one was held accountable.

At this time, the African American press was thriving. It spoke out about the injustices that occurred in the North and South. Despite the fact that newspaper offices were torched and black editors were threatened, the African American press was not silenced. By contrast, many white newspapers reveled in writing lurid and celebratory accounts of the torture and murder of blacks. Even newspapers that opposed lynchings often implied that a victim was guilty of some crime.

In the next chapter, we will look at the lives of the courageous African American newsmen and newswomen who stood up to this system of racial oppression. In the face of threats and insults, they spoke out for justice and human rights. Their voices could not be silenced, and through their efforts, they reshaped American society to be fairer and more just for all.

Frederick Douglass, escaped slave and famed orator and author

The Storytellers

Through centuries of injustice, many African American journalists took up the banner of liberty and equal rights. Their personal stories and work are fascinating topics. The challenges they faced changed depending on the era in which they lived. Yet from slavery to segregation, they were persecuted and harassed by their opponents and often the government itself. Though their stories differ, what unites these writers is their tireless drive to better the United States and lift up the oppressed and marginalized in society.

Frederick Douglass

The most prominent and well-known African American of the nineteenth century was undoubtedly Frederick Douglass. He devoted his life to campaigning for justice and equality—not just for African Americans, but also for women and Native Americans. In the United States, he was a leader of the abolitionist movement, and his writings were known around the world.

Douglass was born into slavery in Maryland around the year 1818. Like most people born into slavery, he never knew his own birthday. In his autobiography, he reflects on the fact that "it is the wish of most masters … to keep their slaves thus ignorant," as well as on the anguish this caused him as a child.

Unlike most slaves, Douglass learned to read and write as a youth. Slaveholders considered education too dangerous for slaves. However, a kind mistress began teaching Douglass at one point. When Douglass's master found out, he demanded his wife cease the lessons and delivered a speech about the dangers of education for slaves. This speech convinced Douglass that he needed to learn to read and write. After that, Douglass traded his food to white children who lived nearby for reading lessons. Later, he would run a Sunday school and teach other slaves to read and write.

Douglass was determined to escape from slavery and live as a freeman. In 1836, Douglass plotted to run away with a group of slaves. However, they were betrayed by a fellow slave and could not put their plan into action.

Two years later, Douglass tried again. This time, he went alone. A free African American he knew gave Douglass his identification papers. However, the physical description did not match Douglass at all. Upon close inspection, there was no doubt his deception would be discovered. Nevertheless, Douglass disguised himself as a sailor and boarded a train heading north. The conductor only glanced at Douglass's papers, and he was on his way toward freedom. As he rode the train, he saw several people who knew him—and knew he was not a free sailor. Luckily, they failed to recognize him. Decades later, he would write that he suspected one German blacksmith he knew well did realize his deception but did not betray him.

At the age of twenty, Douglass had escaped from slavery. He later wrote about his feeling at the time:

> I have been frequently asked how I felt when I found myself in a free State. I have never been able to answer the question with any satisfaction to myself. It was a moment of the highest excitement I ever experienced. I suppose I felt as one may imagine the unarmed mariner to feel when he is rescued by a friendly man-of-war from the pursuit of a pirate. In writing to a dear friend, immediately after my arrival at New York, I said I felt like one who had escaped a den of hungry lions. This state of mind, however, very soon subsided; and I was again seized with a feeling of great insecurity and loneliness. I was yet liable to be taken back, and subjected to all the tortures of slavery.

A freeman, Douglass became involved with the abolitionist movement. He subscribed to William Lloyd Garrison's newspaper, the *Liberator*, and later wrote that it "took a place in my heart second only to the Bible." Douglass began giving abolitionist speeches. In 1845, he published his first autobiography, *Narrative of the Life of Frederick Douglass, an American Slave.* It became popular around the world, and Douglass went on speaking tours across the United States and Europe.

In 1847, Douglass began publishing his own abolitionist newspaper, the *North Star.* It was later called *Frederick Douglass' Paper.* The motto of the paper was "Right is of no sex—Truth is of no color—God is the Father of us all, and we are brethren." This was a remarkably forward-thinking sentiment in a country where women could not vote and slavery flourished. Douglass continued to publish the paper until 1859, when he fled the United States due to the arrest of John Brown. Brown had letters from Douglass in his possession, and Douglass feared this would lead to his arrest and a show trial about his involvement in the raid on Harpers Ferry.

With the end of slavery in 1865, Douglass continued to campaign for equal rights for both African Americans and women. He published and spoke out against the injustices after Reconstruction in the South, as well as prejudice in the North. He died in 1895 at the age of seventy-seven. His career as an abolitionist and proponent for equal rights had stretched more than fifty years. Born into slavery, he witnessed the end of the evil institution, the hope for equal rights in the years after the Civil War, and the end of that hope with the beginning of Jim Crow across the South. Nonetheless, his voice defined the period he lived in and still serves as an example of the change that one man committed to justice can inspire across the globe.

The Back-to-Africa Controversy

The question of whether African Americans should seek to emigrate to Africa has a long history in the United States. Some of the earliest attempts to resettle black Americans to Africa were spearheaded by white Americans. In some cases, their motives were undoubtedly racist. They did not care about the well-being of free African Americans—only the fact that they would be removed from the United States. Other whites had kinder motives. Given the intense racism and inequality of the times, they believed there was no hope for justice toward African Americans in the United States. As a result, emigration to Africa was their best option.

The African American community and press were divided on the question of returning to Africa. It was a point of contention for more than 150 years between the early 1800s and the civil rights movement of the 1960s. Some disillusioned African Americans, like Marcus Garvey, believed there was little future for blacks in the United States and saw emigration as their best option. In Africa, they would be able to create a nation of their own. Alternatively, other leading intellectuals, like W. E. B. Du Bois, believed that African Americans should focus on winning civil rights in the United States.

The split over African emigration was apparent in the African American press from its earliest days. The very first newspaper owned and operated by African Americans—*Freedom's Journal*—was brought low by the controversy. One of the two founders—John Russwurm—supported the efforts of the white-led American Colonization Society to return blacks to Africa, while the other founder—Samuel Cornish—did not. Cornish resigned because of the disagreement. When the paper publicly declared its support for emigration, its readership declined to the point that the newspaper went out of business. Russwurm emigrated to Liberia soon afterward. There he started another newspaper, the *Liberia Herald*.

W. E. B. Du Bois lived from 1868 to 1963. He died in Ghana after leaving the United States.

W. E. B. Du Bois

With the rise of segregation after the Civil War, there was a divide among African Americans about how to move forward. One side, led by Booker T. Washington, championed an approach of accommodation. Washington made a deal with prominent white Southerners. In return for basic rights like education in the South, African Americans would not fight against segregation and disenfranchisement.

W. E. B. Du Bois took the opposite approach. He denounced Washington and his deal with white Southerners. Instead, he wanted African Americans to organize and protest for civil rights. Born in 1868, just after the end of the Civil War, Du Bois became the first African American to earn a PhD from Harvard University in 1895. He became one of the most prominent African Americans of his generation and spent his life campaigning to end segregation, lynchings, and disenfranchisement.

In 1909, Du Bois helped found the National Association for the Advancement of Colored People (NAACP). The organization was founded in response to the Springfield race riot of 1908. The Illinois race riot began after a white woman accused a black man of sexual assault. (The accuser later admitted the incident had never happened.) A white mob gathered and began to methodically burn black businesses and houses across the city. Two black men were lynched. One was shot while defending his home. The other was an eighty-four-year-old man who was targeted for his thirty-year marriage to a white woman. Thousands of African

Americans fled their homes in terror as the mob looted and burned its way across the city.

In 1910, Du Bois became the NAACP's director of publicity and research. In that role, he founded the official magazine of the NAACP, the *Crisis*. In its first issue, he outlined the purpose of the magazine, to "show the danger of race prejudice" and "stand for the rights of men, irrespective of color or race, for the highest ideals of American democracy, and for reasonable but earnest and persistent attempts to gain these rights and realize these ideals."

Du Bois was the editor of the *Crisis* for twenty-four years and helped make it one of the most important publications of the African American press. His opinions molded the direction of the magazine.

After its founding, the NAACP spent the next half century fighting against Jim Crow and discrimination. Its members organized protests and boycotts. They also used the courts to try to strike down unjust laws. It was the leading organization during the civil rights movement of the 1950s and 1960s that finally won the right to vote for African Americans across the United States. Today, the organization continues to fight against injustice. The *Crisis* is still published, and Du Bois's unapologetic demand for equal rights echoes in its pages.

Ida B. Wells-Barnett

Ida B. Wells-Barnett was a famous antilynching activist and journalist. She was born into slavery in 1862 before being freed as a young child with the end of the institution in

Ida B. Wells-Barnett lived from 1862 to 1931.

The Birth of a Nation

In 1915, the film *The Birth of a Nation* (originally titled *The Clansman*) was released in the United States. It was a hopelessly racist film. White actors in blackface portrayed African Americans who conformed to ridiculous stereotypes. The film was also supposed to be based on historical fact, but it attempted to rewrite history. The Ku Klux Klan (KKK), a racist organization that aimed to oppress and terrorize African Americans, was portrayed as heroic.

The Birth of a Nation became immensely popular and received praise from all corners of American society, including the US government. In fact, it was the first film to be screened at the White House. President Woodrow Wilson reportedly said, "It's like writing history with lightning. My only regret is that it is all so terribly true." While scholars debate if he said these exact words, he certainly shared the sentiment. Newspapers around the country lauded the film and its racist ideas. Most wrote that it was historically accurate and did not criticize the film's sanitized portrayal of the KKK.

Conversely, the African American press took a hard line against the film. The NAACP—still in its infancy—organized protests and handed out pamphlets critical of the film. African American newspapers published blistering reviews. One opinion piece published in the *Crisis* expresses what many

During the early 1920s, the KKK operated openly and wielded immense political power.

African Americans around the country doubtlessly felt: "*The Birth of a Nation* is an indefensible libel upon a race, that is nothing less than an indictment of a whole people, the more damning because it purports to be historical and impartial. *The Birth of Nation* is not history; it is travesty. It is not realism; it is an abomination."

the United States. Although free, she and her family faced intense discrimination in their home state of Mississippi.

She moved to Memphis, Tennessee, in 1882 and worked there as a schoolteacher in a segregated school. Two years later, while riding a train, she experienced the violent injustice of segregation. After buying a first-class ticket, she was asked to move to the train car reserved for black people. When she refused, she was physically dragged from the train. Unwilling to submit to the injustice of the times, she sued the train company. Although she won the court case, her victory was overturned on appeal. The incident on the train inspired her to begin her career as a journalist. She wrote for various papers before becoming a co-owner of the *Free Speech*—a local newspaper in Memphis.

In 1892, there was high-profile lynching in Memphis. A group of three African Americans had opened a store in the city. A competing white storeowner gathered a mob and attacked their store in the middle of the night. The three black men fought back, and three white citizens were killed. The African American men were arrested, but before they could stand trial, they were taken from the jail and lynched.

Wells-Barnett wrote impassioned pieces denouncing the lynching in Memphis. She began writing about other lynchings occurring in the South as well. Her writings antagonized many whites around the country who supported the practice of racial violence and the terror that it caused among African Americans. One night later that year, the offices of the *Free Speech* were destroyed by a white mob. Luckily, Wells-Barnett was in New York at the time and was not injured in the attack.

Wells-Barnett was forced to move to the North for her own safety. From there, she continued to write about lynchings and to argue passionately for an end to the segregation and injustice that African Americans across the country faced. She was a founding member of the NAACP and did much to advance the causes of African Americans. She founded the first kindergarten for black children in Chicago. Additionally, she was a part of the women's suffrage movement that sought to win the right to vote for women in the United States. Until her death in 1931 at the age of sixty-eight, she never stopped campaigning for justice.

Robert Sengstacke Abbott

One newsman who would come to define the African American press was born on the little island of Saint Simons off the coast of Georgia. From these humble roots, Robert Sengstacke Abbott went on to become a millionaire and shape the history of one of America's most important cities: Chicago.

Abbott was born in 1868 to two former slaves who had just recently been freed due to the end of the Civil War. However, his father soon died, and his mother remarried a Savannah man who had recently returned from Germany. Abbott's stepfather moved the family to the suburbs of Savannah, where Abbott would spend his childhood.

Abbott attended Hampton Institute in Virginia to study printing as a young man, before going to Chicago and studying law at Kent College of Law. Because of racial discrimination, he found it impossible to be successful as a lawyer. This forced him to look to printing to support himself.

In 1905, Abbott founded the *Chicago Defender* in his landlord's kitchen with an investment of just twenty-five cents. The newspaper grew rapidly and became a cornerstone of the African American press. The *Chicago Defender* owed some of its success to its flashy style. This was based partly on the yellow journalism that thrived at the turn of the twentieth century. New York papers run by the famous newsmen Joseph Pulitzer and William Randolph Hearst competed for readers by running exaggerated headlines and graphic stories. The *Chicago Defender* copied their use of attention-grabbing headlines and bold, red ink. Graphic accounts and photos of the violence African Americans were subject to were also included in the paper. This marked a shift in the African American press from a more restrained style to one that was more truthful about the grisly facts of lynchings and racial violence.

The *Chicago Defender* was extremely successful as a business due to these techniques. But it was also fearless in its championing of African American issues and greater justice in the United States. It urged African Americans suffering under Jim Crow in the South to make the journey north. Its tone was unapologetic and forceful. One antilynching slogan it used was "If you must die, take at least one with you." Words like "negro," "colored," and "black" did not occur in its pages. "The Race" was its preferred term, and African Americans were called "Race men" and "Race women."

Abbott grew wealthy with his paper's success. His influence spread from Chicago across the entire United States, along with copies of his paper. He died in 1940, but the *Chicago Defender* continued under the leadership of his nephew. It still exists today.

Marcus Garvey

Marcus Garvey was a controversial figure and remains controversial in the present day. He was convicted of mail fraud in the United States, although many doubt the validity of the charges. His views were uncompromising and pitted him against most figures of his time, both African American and white. However, there is no doubt that he inspired a generation of African Americans to be fiercely proud of their race and heritage.

Garvey was born in Jamaica in 1887. At the time, Jamaica was a British colony—although most of its population was black. The ancestors of black Jamaicans had been brought to the island as slaves to do the backbreaking labor of growing and harvesting sugarcane in the tropical heat. Garvey apprenticed as a printer when he was a boy before traveling the world. He lived in Central America and Europe, witnessing firsthand the exploitation of much of the world by Europe for economic gain. At the time, virtually all of Africa was divided between the European powers and exploited for its natural resources.

Marcus Garvey's legacy is celebrated around the globe. This monument stands in Trinidad and Tobago.

In 1916, Garvey moved to the United States. Two years previously he had founded the Universal Negro Improvement and Conservation Association and African Communities League (often shortened to Universal Negro Improvement Association, or UNIA). The UNIA fought for the civil rights of blacks across the world. It was also an early promoter of black nationalism: the idea that blacks should actively cultivate a culture separate from whites and not seek to assimilate into white culture. The UNIA also encouraged the migration of blacks from the United States back to Africa, where independent black states would one day rise from colonial rule. These views were not always popular with other black leaders, who believed that African Americans should focus on expanding civil rights in the United States rather than leave.

Garvey founded the newspaper *Negro World* in 1918 to act as the voice of the UNIA. Membership in the UNIA skyrocketed at the time due to a huge uptick in racial violence. In 1919, the events that would become known as the Red Summer came to pass. Lynchings took place across the United States, and race riots broke out in many cities. Hundreds of blacks were killed, and the uncompromising ideology of Garvey won millions of supporters.

Garvey was the most popular black leader for a short time. However, he soon fell from grace. Garvey founded a shipping company to encourage trade and migration between the United States, Africa, and the Caribbean. The business failed, and Garvey was sentenced to five years in

Joseph McCarthy (*center*) targeted notable African Americans
and civil rights organizations in his anticommunist witch-hunt.

prison for mail fraud related to selling stock in the business. The charges were the result of an FBI infiltration of the movement. The government was bitterly opposed to its message. Garvey's popularity waned after the scandal, and a new president of the UNIA was elected. Garvey was later deported to Jamaica. He died years later in relative obscurity in London, although he is now a celebrated—if controversial—figure.

Charlotta Bass

Born in South Carolina in 1880, Charlotta Bass moved to California in 1910. She settled in Los Angeles and soon got a job at a local African American–owned newspaper called the *Owl*. When the owner of that newspaper, John J. Neimore, died in 1912, Bass became the owner and editor. She renamed the paper the *California Eagle*.

Bass used the newspaper to fight for social change in California

The Brotherhood of Sleeping Car Porters was an early union for African American workers.

and across the United States. She published articles on a wide range of issues, from discrimination to lynchings and the Ku Klux Klan. The Klan even took her to court for libel at one point, but she won the case. Later, when she campaigned to be on the city council, the Klan sent her death threats.

The *California Eagle* coordinated a number of social campaigns. For instance, Bass strongly supported a movement to shop at African American–owned, or at least integrated, businesses in California. The newspaper spread awareness of the campaign with the slogan "Don't Shop Where You Can't Work."

Bass was also closely involved with many other groups fighting for greater rights for African Americans. She was a member of the NAACP as well as a high-ranking local member of Marcus Garvey's UNIA. She also spearheaded movements of her own. She started the Home Protective Association that sought to end housing covenants, discriminative practices that excluded African Americans from living in many areas.

Like Garvey and many other African American leaders of the era, Bass came under intense scrutiny from law enforcement and the federal government. She was put under surveillance by the FBI. She was also accused of being a communist during the political witch-hunts of the McCarthy era. Like many other people at the time, her fight for social justice was used to demonize her and ruin her good name.

After nearly forty years of management, Bass sold the *California Eagle* in 1951. However, she stayed active in politics and the fight against injustice. In 1952, she campaigned to be vice president of the United States on the ticket of the Progressive Party. This made her the first African American woman to run for national office.

A. Philip Randolph

The strong ties between the African American press and the civil rights movement of the 1950s and 1960s are embodied in A. Philip Randolph. Born in Florida in 1889, Randolph cofounded the magazine the *Messenger* as a young man. Later, he became one of the most important leaders of the civil rights movement that finally led to the Voting Rights Act of 1965.

Randolph's interest in the struggle for civil rights began after reading a book by W. E. B. Du Bois. Soon after, he met a black socialist by the name of Chandler Owen. Their first venture together was founding an

A. Philip Randolph's contributions to the civil
rights movement are widely celebrated.

employment agency for African Americans. Their later work together had a much greater impact. After the United States entered World War I in 1917, the two founded the *Messenger*. In its pages, they urged African Americans to avoid service in the armed forces. They did not think the war in Europe concerned African Americans who were being oppressed and persecuted in their homeland. This stance put them at odds with many African American leaders at the time who saw the patriotic service of African Americans as a necessary first step to argue for more civil rights. The *Messenger* also served as a platform for articles that denounced lynchings and Jim Crow.

The *Messenger* only lasted eleven years, but Randolph continued fighting for equality. In 1925, he helped start the Brotherhood of Sleeping Car Porters (BSCP)—the first major African American labor union. He helped head the union for the next forty years and successfully fought for it and other black unions to gain more rights.

Randolph used his influence to lead several major campaigns for civil rights. In 1941, he called for a protest march in Washington, DC, unless President Franklin D. Roosevelt finally agreed to end discriminatory hiring in the federal government. Despite being pressured to call off the march, he stood firm. Finally, Roosevelt caved to Randolph's demands before the march occurred. Likewise, in 1946, Randolph began lobbying for an end to segregation in the armed forces. President Harry S. Truman issued an executive order desegregating all branches of the armed forces as a result.

But Randolph's most famous work in civil rights was likely the 1963 March on Washington for Jobs and Freedom, which he helped to organize. On that day, Martin Luther King Jr.—one of the few civil rights leaders of equal stature to Randolph—delivered his "I Have a Dream" speech from the steps of the Lincoln Memorial. The event is credited with the passage of the Civil Rights Act of 1964 and the Voting Rights Act of 1965. These laws finally ended the era of racial discrimination, disenfranchisement, and segregation that had characterized African American life for the previous hundred years since the end of the Civil War.

African American newspapers like the *Pittsburgh Courier* were distributed across the country.

Stories of Resistance

The history of the African American press has stretched nearly two centuries. Throughout that time, the focus of the publications has changed depending on the challenges of the era. But there has often been a common theme across the many publications that belong to the African American press. Issues of injustice and oppression are covered again and again. While the nature of the injustice has changed with American society, African American journalists and activists have fulfilled the role of society's moral conscience in many ways. They have argued persuasively not only for more racial justice but also for justice for women and other minorities.

The Opening Salvo

Freedom's Journal, which began in 1827, was the first newspaper in the United States to be owned and operated by African Americans. Its first issue began by justifying the need for an African American press. The paper's editors explain:

> We wish to plead our own cause. Too long have others spoken for us. Too long has the publick [*sic*] been deceived by misrepresentations, in things which concern us dearly, though in the estimation of some mere trifles; for though there are many in society who exercise towards us benevolent feelings; still (with sorrow we confess it) there are others who make it their business to enlarge upon the least trifle, which tends to the discredit of any person of colour; and pronounce anathemas and denounce our whole body for the misconduct of this guilty one. We are aware that there are many instances of vice among us, but we avow that it is because no one has taught its subjects to be virtuous; many instances of poverty, because no sufficient efforts accommodated to minds contracted by slavery, and deprived of early education have been made, to teach them how to husband their hard earnings, and to secure to themselves comfort … The civil rights of a people being of the greatest value, it shall ever be our duty to vindicate our brethren, when oppressed; and to lay the case before the publick. We shall also urge upon our brethren, (who are qualified by the laws of the different states) the expediency of using their elective franchise; and of making an independent use of the same.

The purpose of the newspaper is laid out in detail. It is a platform for African Americans to speak for themselves, rather than to depend on white abolitionists and allies. It is a means to defend the reputation of all African Americans from the slander of the white press of the time. Additionally, it is a means to encourage change by challenging public opinion and through the ballot box.

It is notable that *Freedom's Journal* advocated for change through elective franchise—or voting. Despite the abomination of slavery, with its inherent racial violence and injustice, no violent response is called for. Rather, the paper says it is up to African Americans to combat the attitudes of the time and to use what rights they are afforded to peacefully seek change.

These aims outlined above would not be restricted to *Freedom's Journal*. Later African American–owned newspapers would largely follow the same lofty ideals. Even today, the African American press is often needed to combat harmful stereotypes that shape mainstream media coverage.

The Outrage of Slavery

As you might expect, one of the early focuses of the African American press was the institution of slavery. Arguments against slavery were often found in the pages of newspaper, but they were also published in pamphlets. Pamphlets were a common type of literature in early American history. They allowed ideas to be disseminated easily and cheaply. This genre includes the famous work *Common Sense* by Thomas Paine, which argued

Pamphlets afforded African Americans a platform to publish their views.

WALKER'S

APPEAL,

With a Brief Sketch of his Life.

BY

HENRY HIGHLAND GARNET.

AND ALSO

GARNET'S ADDRESS

TO THE SLAVES OF THE UNITED STATES OF AMERICA.

NEW-YORK:
Printed by J. H. Tobitt, 9 Spruce-st.
1848

persuasively for an independent United States during the American Revolution. (Early on, the revolution was not truly a war of independence.)

African American authors penned and distributed pamphlets before the first African American newspaper was even published. But one of the most famous pamphlets was published in 1829. Named *Walker's Appeal*, it was a fiercely critical attack on the institution of slavery—as well as the United States and the many European powers that still supported it.

David Walker was born a freeman in Wilmington, North Carolina, but he saw the horrors of slavery there. He eventually resettled in Boston, where he wrote his influential pamphlet. In it, he argues that "we, (coloured people of these United States of America) are the most wretched, degraded and abject set of beings that ever lived since the world began, and that the white Americans having reduced us to the wretched state of slavery, treat us in that condition more cruel (they being an enlighted and Christian people), than any heathen nation did any people whom it had reduced to our condition." He gives many examples of pre-Christian nations that treated their slaves much more humanely than the United States in his day.

Walker's portrayal of white Americans—and his attack on their Christian morality—won him few friends. Southern states tried to stop his pamphlet from being distributed. Georgia offered a $10,000 reward for his capture (despite the fact he was a freeman) or a $1,000 reward for his death.

African Americans suffered racism on a regular basis in New York in the 1700s and 1800s.

In his pamphlet, Walker also urges slaves to seek their own freedom. He writes, "Never make an attempt to gain our freedom or natural right from under our cruel oppressors and murderers, until you see your way clear— when that hour arrives and you move, be not afraid or dismayed." Walker's uncompromising opposition to slavery alienated not only Southerners but also many white abolitionists and other free African Americans. Many other antislavery works were not as forceful in their condemnation of whites. Many also focused on lawful change through voting and the political process rather than through escape.

With the end of slavery, the antislavery works that had previously been a large body of literature ceased to be published. However, there was then a new set of problems that came to the forefront for African Americans. Disenfranchisement, segregation, and discrimination characterized daily life in the South, as well as in parts of the North.

Response to the White Press

For its entire history, the African American press has devoted significant effort to rebutting the racism and stereotypes of some segments of society. In the early days, this pitted black newspapers against virtually every other publication in the United States, other than some white abolitionist writings. The treatment of blacks in typical newspapers—in both the North and South—was savage. Black people were not given the consideration due to human beings and were mocked and belittled at length.

One article in the *New York Times*—a paper that is typically forward-thinking and would later champion some civil rights issues—is representative of the times. Published in 1837, it reads:

> Yesterday afternoon, a stout negro hailed an omnibus that was passing up Broadway, and attempted to get in. The driver turning his head, and observing the color of his new passenger, jumped up, in great fury, and flourished his whip high in the air, threatening the negro with a sound flogging if he did not instantly retire. The latter did not seem much disposed to follow such advice, but the whipcord coming in fearful contiguity with his ears, he reluctantly retired, threatening the driver with an action at law, Coachee shook his whip in defiance—the negro shook his head, and the bystanders shook their sides with laughter.

A response to the article was published in the *Colored American*. It was aptly titled "They Glory in Their Shame":

> Did we not fear it would be casting pearl before swine, we would rebuke, severely, the whole posse of the above, the editor, the driver, and the merry-making bystanders.
>
> Are these thoughtless men without human souls? or do they think there is no righteous God, before whom they are accountable? Men who can chronicle, with approbation, or laugh at such oppressive, BRUTAL DOINGS as the above, must be lost to the feeling of sympathy and humanity, without which, a man is A MERE ANIMAL, worse than dead while he lives.
>
> We envy not the American, who at this enlightened day, can look with approbation on such scenes. Is it not enough, that we have dragged in chains, the poor colored man from his native home, and exuded from his blood and bones, millions of treasures, without making him any reward. Shall we be so narrow-souled, so FIENDLIKE, as after having ruined a fellowbeing, to add insult, and to make merry over his sufferings?

The horrifyingly racist attitudes of the white press were not always so plain to see. Sometimes, they were under the surface of the writing. Many authors tried to

Seneca Falls, New York, was the site of the first convention for women's rights.

portray themselves as allies of African Americans while simultaneously implying that African Americans could not be expected to know what was best for themselves and therefore needed to be guided and controlled.

African American newspapers often made great efforts to dispel theses racist attitudes published by white authors and editors. African American publications also had to publish accurate stories on many incidents that were distorted by mainstream newspapers. For instance, lynchings and race riots were often minimized by other sources. It was usually implied that the murdered African Americans deserved their fate in some way due to allegations that would clearly never hold up in a fair court of law. It was left to the African American press to give a more objective account of the facts in such cases.

Alliance with Women

The African American press was not exclusively concerned with issues of race. Prominent black leaders also lent their voices to other social issues of their times. One of the most important social movements of the nineteenth century was the women's suffrage movement. Suffrage is the right to vote. For much of American history, women did not have this right.

In 1848, the Seneca Falls Convention was held in New York. It was the first women's rights convention of its kind. At this meeting, it was decided that securing the right to vote should be a major aim of the movement. For the next seventy-two years, women actively advocated and protested for greater political rights, especially the right to vote. Finally, in 1920, the Nineteenth Amendment was passed. It prohibits the federal and state governments from denying the right to vote based on a person's sex. Of course, the disenfranchisement of black women continued via Jim Crow in many places.

Frederick Douglass was one black leader who supported women's suffrage from an early date. He attended the Seneca Falls Convention and soon after published an editorial in the *North Star* supporting their goals. He wrote:

> We are free to say that in respect to political rights, we hold woman to be justly entitled to all we claim for man. We go farther, and express our conviction that all political rights that it is expedient for man to exercise, it is equally so for woman. All that distinguishes man as an intelligent and accountable being, is equally true of woman; and if that government only is just which governs by the free consent of the governed, there can be no reason in the world for denying to woman the exercise of the elective franchise, or a hand in making and administering the laws of the land. Our doctrine is that "right is of no sex."

Today, these words do not appear controversial. But at the time that Douglass published them, many people

The Arteries
of America

The distribution of African American publications was often fraught with difficulties. They were typically not well received in the South, and some states even tried to prevent their sale. This was especially true during the Great Migration of the early twentieth century. As millions of African Americans left the oppressive atmosphere of the South during Jim Crow for the North, white Southerners tried to stem their flow so that they still had access to cheap labor. They did this by attacking the newspapers that encouraged them to leave.

One way that states tried to prevent the distribution of African Americans newspapers was by banning their distribution by mail. This presented a serious problem for African Americans in the South who wanted to read popular newspapers printed in the North. However, the *Chicago Defender* came up with an ingenious solution to this problem. It recruited black railroad porters—servers and baggage handlers—to sell the paper in person around the South. In fact, A. Philip Randolph's labor union, the Brotherhood of Sleeping Car Porters, was especially important to this movement. They sold copies of the *Chicago Defender* across the Southern states.

The railroads that connected the United States like a vast system of arteries and veins were critical to African American history during this period. They helped distribute the *Chicago Defender* across the South and brought African Americans fleeing Jim Crow to the North.

did not believe women should have equal rights. Douglass himself would die decades before women finally won the right to vote in 1920. However, he and other black leaders continuously fought to see that women, too, could vote after African Americans won that right in 1870.

Black Nationalism

The African American press was also a key force in fostering black pride. After centuries of slavery and constant abuse in the white press, it was difficult for African Americans to see their diversity as an asset. Many black intellectuals used newspapers and other publications to argue that this should not be the case. African Americans had been victimized and stereotyped, black newspapers said, but they ought to feel no shame as a result. It was the immorality of the slave owners and racist political system that should be hated, not African Americans.

As we have seen, Marcus Garvey was one of the most influential black leaders who advocated for greater pride among African Americans. Garvey published an article called "African Fundamentalism" that outlined his views on the subject:

> The time has come for the Negro to forget and cast behind him his hero worship and adoration of other races, and to start out immediately to create and emulate heroes of his own. We must canonize our own saints, create our own martyrs, and elevate to positions of fame and honor black men and women who have made their distinct

contributions to our racial history. Sojourner Truth is worthy of the place of sainthood alongside of Joan of Arc … Africa has produced countless numbers of men and women, in war and in peace, whose luster and bravery outshine that of any other people. Then why not see good and perfection in ourselves? We must inspire a literature and promulgate a doctrine of our own without any apologies to the powers that be. The right is ours and God's. Let contrary sentiment and cross opinions go to the winds. Opposition to race independence is the weapon of the enemy to defeat the hopes of an unfortunate people. We are entitled to our own opinions and not obligated to or bound by the opinions of others.

It was heartfelt, forceful words like these that led Garvey's UNIA to gain millions of members in a short time. Even after his death, Garvey's words would inspire generations of black leaders.

Malcolm X, an influential black leader of the 1950s and 1960s, was born to followers of Garvey. Garvey's views influenced Malcolm X's own black nationalist views. Malcolm X favored a separation of blacks and whites, rather than the idea of integration favored by civil rights leaders like Martin Luther King Jr. and A Philip Randolph.

Miscarriages of Justice

During the Jim Crow era, state courts were often a means to oppress and terrorize African Americans. Throughout the South, African Americans knew that they could be charged with crimes for any reason, whether due to a personal vendetta or the prejudices of a police officer. Once charged, there was no chance of a fair trial. Even in areas with large black populations, juries were typically all white. The fact that a black man was charged was usually taken as all the proof necessary for him to be found guilty. If the case was especially contentious, the accused had to also worry about being dragged from jail and lynched before a verdict was even returned.

One of the most famous court cases of this era was the trial of the "Scottsboro Boys." They were a group of nine African American men and boys who were illegally hitching a ride on a train car in 1931. Police officers found them and removed them from the car, but the officers did not stop there. They found two white women also riding on the train and convinced them to accuse the men of rape. In the ensuing trial, eight of the accused received a death sentence, while one—just thirteen years of age—received life in prison.

The Communist Party rushed to the men's defense, while the NAACP kept its distance. The accusation of rape by a white woman toward black men was extremely contentious, and the NAACP did not wish to be involved with it or the controversial Communist Party. However, like the Communist Party, the African American press rushed to the defense of the nine men. Pointing out the many injustices of the hurried trial, African American newspapers urged that the case be reopened and the NAACP become involved. The *Chicago Defender* published an article criticizing the NAACP and calling for it to "put aside division and bickering and join the effort" to defend the accused men. This was in sharp contrast to the many white newspapers that assumed the men were guilty.

Eventually, the death sentences were overturned, along with some of the convictions. Other men were paroled after lengthy sentences. One man escaped from prison and fled the state—his new home state refused to extradite him. It was not until 2008 that the saga finally ended when Alabama issued three posthumous pardons for the men whose names had not yet been cleared legally.

Unfortunately, cases like this were not uncommon during Jim Crow. The Scottsboro Boys' case was one of the most high-profile instances of racial injustice, due to its inflammatory charges and the fact that one of the women later recanted her entire story and blamed the police for pressuring her to make the accusation. But miscarriages of justice for African Americans were common. White-owned newspapers tended to support the courts and the police rather than question the often shaky evidence or legal proceedings. During Jim Crow, it was left to the African American press to fight for justice for the accused and criticize the racist political system that led to their false imprisonments and executions in all too many cases.

Racial Violence

While courts across the country supported Jim Crow, lawless violence was also used to terrorize and oppress African Americans. Lynchings were often individual acts of violence, while violent events of a massive scale were labeled "race riots." The implication that it was a two-sided conflict, blacks against whites, was generally false. Race riots tended to be the result of white mobs murdering and driving out huge numbers of African Americans from cities. White casualties were frequently only due to self-defense or retaliatory violence after initial rampages by white mobs.

One of the most infamous cases was the East Saint Louis race riot of 1917. Tensions between whites and blacks were high in the city due to labor disputes. After black workers were recruited to replace striking white workers, a white mob marched through a black neighborhood, setting fire to properties and attacking black civilians. Soon after, a group of white men drove through another African American neighborhood and shot into buildings. When a group of armed African Americans gathered to defend their homes, they shot into an unmarked police car that was coming to monitor the situation after mistaking them for the shooters. Two white police officers died.

Protesters marching on behalf of the Scottsboro Boys in 1934

During the East Saint Louis race riot, the National Guard was called in to protect African Americans from white mobs.

Freedom Abroad, Jim Crow at Home

Political cartoons have been a staple of the English-speaking press since the eighteenth century. They are often scathingly critical of the political establishment or individual politicians, although they can also be more supportive of the government. The African American press used political cartoons in much the same way as the white press. Individual cartoonists varied greatly in what message they conveyed with their cartoons. Many pointed out the injustice of segregation and discrimination using dark humor.

During World War II, political cartoons drawn by African Americans portrayed the war in different lights. Some cartoonists supported the American war effort. They extolled the virtues of victory gardens and war bonds that the US government was trying to promote at the time. However, other cartoonists used the war as a backdrop for criticism. White politicians who supported Jim Crow at home but denounced the racism of the Nazi government abroad were an easy target for savage political cartoons.

One cartoon by Jan Jackson is representative of this critical genre. It depicts two soldiers labeled "liberation forces" crossing the Atlantic. They are on their way to rescue a chained white woman labeled "enslaved Europe." They leave behind a chained black woman in the United States. The cartoon is captioned "We'll Be Back," and one soldier leers over his shoulder at the black woman. It is a stinging critique of the spirit of the times.

A white mob gathered to avenge them and began a rampage of violence and terror. The *Crisis* published an article detailing the results of the mob violence:

> A mob of white men, women and children burned and destroyed at least $400,000 worth of property belonging to both whites and Negroes; drove 6,000 Negroes out of their homes; and deliberately murdered by shooting, burning and hanging, between one and two hundred human beings who were black.

It fell to the African American press to detail the horrors of the riot. They published accounts of the unimaginable violence that involved the murder of black women and children who were unlucky enough to be caught by the mob.

On the other hand, white newspapers tended to focus on the initial slaying of the two white policemen. Some even published stories about how lucky it was the National Guard broke up the "race riot" before blacks could retaliate against whites for the horrible violence they suffered.

Segregation and Discrimination

In addition to race riots and outrageous acts of violence, the African American press focused on the mundane acts of discrimination that characterized life for African Americans throughout the period of segregation. While segregation was most intense in the South, it also existed

A movie theater for African Americans in 1939

throughout much of the North. Housing covenants barred blacks from living in large sections of most Northern cities. This forced them into overcrowded districts where living conditions were poor. Segregation in schools and at work existed throughout much of the North. Under President Woodrow Wilson, even the agencies of the federal government were segregated.

The African American press challenged these racist institutions that affected their lives. They advocated for greater equality and often encouraged African Americans to make their voices heard in the fight against injustice.

Between the Civil War and the end of the civil rights movement nearly a century later, countless campaigns were spearheaded by the black press. One of the biggest was the *Pittsburgh Courier*'s Double V campaign. The name is a reference to the "V for victory" campaign that was used by the Allies during World War II. The campaign was started by a twenty-six-year-old cafeteria worker who wrote a letter to the *Pittsburgh Courier*, which was then the largest black newspaper:

> The V for victory sign is being displayed prominently in all so-called democratic countries which are fighting for victory over aggression, slavery and tyranny. If this V sign means that to those now engaged in this great conflict, then let we colored Americans adopt the double VV for a double victory. The first V for victory over our enemies from without, the second V for victory over our enemies from within. For surely those who

perpetuate these ugly prejudices here are seeking to destroy our democratic form of government just as surely as the Axis forces.

The newspaper promoted the campaign for months. It published pictures of African Americans from around the country displaying the double V sign with their fingers (now more widely known as the peace sign). In the end, prejudice was not defeated in the United States, but it was a forerunner of the civil rights movement that would eventually win key rights for African Americans across the United States.

Around 250,000 people heard Martin Luther King Jr.'s "I Have A Dream" speech.

The Power of Truth and Dignity

The nearly two-hundred-year history of the African American press is full of change. From slavery, to segregation, to the hard-won victories of the civil rights movement, the African American press has shaped American history. We have looked at many of the themes covered by the African American press throughout its existence. In this chapter, we will see the effects of that coverage. From the civil rights movement to Black Lives Matter, the press has been an important tool for social change and a platform for black voices.

Creating a Black Community

The institution of slavery sought to prevent the creation of a black community. It prevented African Americans from learning how to read or write. Many areas banned the assembly of slaves outside of church, and families were routinely broken up when family members were sold as slaves. Early on, slaves often did not even have much in common with other slaves. They rarely spoke the same African language and were similar in little else than their skin color.

The population of free blacks—and later the millions of slaves emancipated after the Civil War—had to forge their own ties of community. The African American press took a leading role in creating a robust and thriving black community in the United States. Local papers printed the ordinary sort of information that binds a community together: birth announcements, lists of graduates, and obituaries. These were lacking from mainstream newspapers that published this information only for white readers. Ads for black businesses and events were disseminated in black publications as well. This alone went a long way toward the creation of local communities.

Without the African American press, there would have been no record of the lives of the many black Americans over the years. But the African American press also took a more direct role in the forging of a black national identity. It actively debated how black people fit into American society. Oppressed and marginalized, black intellectuals published articles debating how to live in such an untenable situation.

Scholar Todd Vogel explains how this creation of a black community changed over the years:

> After Emancipation, free blacks in the South created scores of black newspapers to stitch freedmen into the community and protect their

rights. The early twentieth-century black press sought to define itself and its community amid American modernism. Midcentury writers analyzed the impact of international events, like the growth of fascism, on America's black community. Writers in the 1960s took on the task of defining revolution in that decade's ferment.

Throughout history, it was the black press that took the lead. The result is the strong sense of black national identity and culture that exists today.

The Great Migration

One of the earliest successes of the African American press was in the Great Migration. Between 1916 and 1970, an estimated six million African Americans moved from the South to the North. This fundamentally altered life not only for the vast number of people who moved but also for residents of major cities across the North. Cities that had once been largely white, like Chicago, New York, Pittsburgh, and Detroit, grew to have large populations of black citizens. Rather than celebrate this diversity, many white residents responded with violence and hate. But this did not stem the tide of migrants who could no longer bear life under Jim Crow and wanted greater economic opportunities and freedom.

In one of the more extreme examples, the population of Detroit went from just 1 percent black in 1910 to more than 80 percent black today. Similar shifts were seen in many major cities across the North to a lesser extent.

Percentage of African American population living in the American South

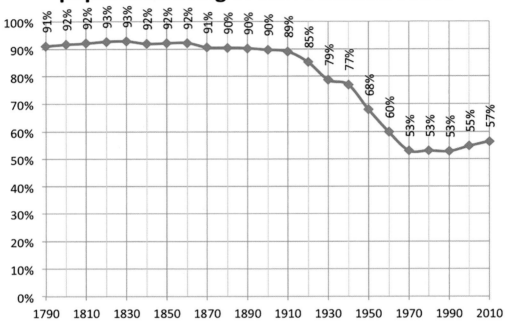

Between 1916 and 1970, six million African Americans moved from the South to the North during the Great Migration.

The Great Migration had many causes. Life in the South was extraordinarily hard for blacks with the heavy-handed systems of racial segregation as well as lynchings, disenfranchisement, poor public education, and few well-paying jobs. Furthermore, the American entrance into World War I in 1917 led to the growth of factory jobs in the North. At the same time, many factory workers were away in the armed forces. Their absence meant Southern blacks could expect much better paying work if they made their way North.

The *Chicago Defender* was also a key factor in the early years of the Great Migration. The paper campaigned relentlessly for Southern African Americans to come North. It printed job advertisements in its pages, as well as train schedules to let blacks in the South know when they could make the trip North. It denounced the racial injustices of the South while praising how much better life was in the North. When Southern states banned the sale of the paper by mail, it worked with black train porters to continue its circulation. The results were staggering. In 1910, 89 percent of blacks lived in the South. By 1930, at the urging of the *Chicago Defender*, that number had fallen to 79 percent.

The importance of the Great Migration in American history was monumental. According to scholar James N. Gregory, "Apart from the introduction of automobiles, it would be hard to think of anything that more dramatically reshaped America's big cities in the twentieth century than the relocation of the nation's black population." It was a major reason for the growth of American suburbs. As

Langston Hughes, a leading figure of the Harlem Renaissance and famous author

African Americans settled in cities, white residents often left to live outside in exclusively white areas.

The Great Migration had a huge impact on life for African Americans in many Northern cities. On the one hand, the influx of African Americans from the South often led to heightened racial tensions and violence. It was not a coincidence that the race riots and lynchings of the Red Summer of 1919 occurred a few years into the Great Migration. White residents of Northern cities responded with discrimination, segregation, and violence to the influx of Southern blacks. On the other hand, the Great Migration led to a flowering of black culture in Northern cities. Freed from the terror of Jim Crow, segregation, and a lack of education, African Americans could express themselves to a greater degree.

Harlem, a formerly white neighborhood in New York City, had two hundred thousand black residents by the 1920s. These new residents spurred the Harlem Renaissance, an explosion of artistic innovation among the city's African Americans. Black musicians and writers reinvented their crafts and received national attention. Many figures from this time, like Langston Hughes, are still studied today in schools and universities around the world.

The legacy of the Great Migration was mixed. Those who left the South did escape the heavy hand of Jim Crow. There were greater economic opportunities for blacks in the North, but life there was not without its difficulties. Racial violence, segregation, and discrimination still existed to varying degrees.

According to Pulitzer Prize–winning journalist Isabel Wilkerson:

> The Great Migration would expose the racial divisions and disparities that in many ways continue to plague the nation and dominate headlines today, from police killings of unarmed African-Americans to mass incarceration to widely documented biases in employment, housing, health care and education. Indeed, two of the most tragically recognizable descendants of the Great Migration are Emmett Till, a 14-year-old Chicago boy killed in Mississippi in 1955, and Tamir Rice, a 12-year-old Cleveland boy shot to death by police in 2014 in the city where his ancestors had fled.

The Great Migration did not solve the many injustices that African Americans faced, but it did reshape the cities of the United States.

The Civil Rights Movement

Another of the greatest achievements of the African American press was its important role in the civil rights movement of the 1950s and 1960s. This period resulted in the unraveling of Jim Crow and court-backed segregation in the United States. It ended with the Civil Rights Act of 1964 and the Voting Rights Act of 1965, which finally guaranteed African Americans the right to vote and not be discriminated against. For nearly one hundred years, these rights were given to African Americans by the Fourteenth and Fifteenth Amendments in name but not in practice.

Martin Luther King Jr. was one of the most
famous leaders of the civil rights movement.

Emmett Till's grave features this plaque. Till's murder galvanized the civil rights movement.

The beginning of the civil rights movement is often given as 1954. This is the year of the Supreme Court decision *Brown v. Board of Education of Topeka*. This decision found that the segregation of students in public schools was unconstitutional. In effect, it overturned nearly a century of segregation. Although it applied only to public schools, it set a legal precedent to challenge segregation of all government services. The legal team of the NAACP, which had championed *Brown v. Board of Education*, brought court case after court case against the sprawling system of institutional segregation and discrimination of the 1950s.

Meanwhile, civil rights leaders like Martin Luther King Jr., A. Philip Randolph, and Rosa Parks organized nonviolent resistance to unjust practices. They led boycotts and sit-ins to undermine segregation. Their vision of equality for all was a powerful message that won the support of many white Americans. In this way, they overshadowed the more radical messages of some black leaders who wanted to reject becoming a part of mainstream white society after so many years of oppression.

The African American press played a pivotal role in the civil rights movement, although it did not lead it as it had earlier civil rights campaigns like the Double V campaign. Early on, the civil rights movement received little mainstream press coverage. For example, Martin Luther King's 1955–1956 Montgomery bus boycott, spurred by the arrest of Rosa Parks for refusing to move to the back of a segregated bus, received scant attention in the national news, though it is now considered a seminal event of the civil rights movement. It was

African American publications that helped spread word of the boycott, and this coverage helped rally public support for the cause.

By its end, the civil rights movement was a top story of the mainstream press as well as the African American press. Events like Martin Luther King Jr.'s "I Have a Dream" speech were too big to ignore. Even incidents of racial violence that would once have been overlooked were given more coverage at this time in history.

For example, the lynching of Emmett Till, a fourteen-year-old African American boy, by two white men in Mississippi received national coverage. Accused of whistling at a white woman, Till was beaten and shot. His body was tied to a piece of machinery with barbed wire and dumped in a river. It was a mobilizing incident in the civil rights movement after the African American–owned magazine *Jet* published pictures of Till's body in his open casket on its cover. The two murderers were acquitted by a local jury, although they later received $4,000 to tell the story of their guilt in a magazine. They admitted to the murder but were unapologetic. Even the mainstream press could not help but be outraged by the miscarriage of justice and the horrifying violence of the lynching.

With the success of the civil rights movement in the 1960s, the credit largely went to leaders like Martin Luther King Jr. and the NAACP. However, their extraordinary work was built on the foundation of the African American press. It was a mobilizing force of the movement, and it had helped set the stage by waging a constant war against segregation and injustice for more than a century beforehand.

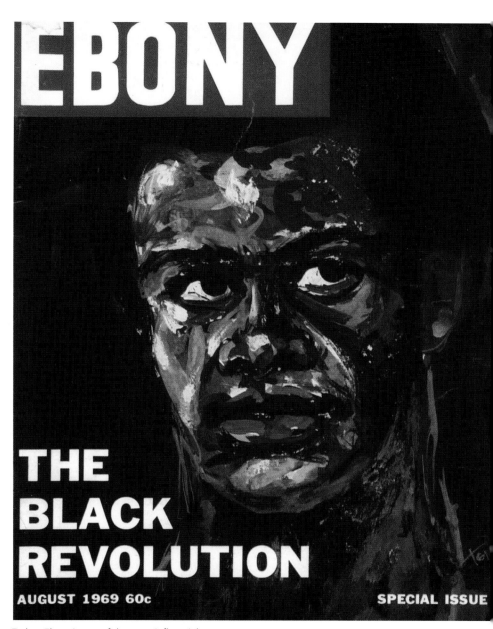

EBONY

THE
BLACK
REVOLUTION

AUGUST 1969 60c

SPECIAL ISSUE

Today, *Ebony* is one of the most influential
publications of the African American press.

The African American Press Today

In the first half of the twentieth century, newspapers like the *Chicago Defender* and *Pittsburgh Courier* regularly sold more than one hundred thousand copies. These papers were then passed around to multiple readers. Today, these newspapers and their successors are lucky to sell ten thousand copies a year. While all newspapers have lost subscribers in recent years, most circulation numbers have not fallen as drastically as those of publications targeting African American readers.

Scholars believe there are a number of factors that have led to this decline, which is often dated back to the 1950s and 1960s. At this time, African American journalists were being hired away from African American publications. With the unraveling of segregation, skilled black journalists could move to the mainstream press for the first time, and this shift happened in large numbers. As a result, black newspapers struggled to remain on the cutting edge.

Additionally, the anticommunist fervor of the time made African American newspapers hold their tongue and criticize society less. The government made examples of people like Charlotta Bass who refused to be silenced. As a result, other newspapers often fell into line. The fact that they no longer spoke as freely meant people had less reason to listen to them.

While the circulation of print newspapers remains low, African American voices have expanded into new domains. Magazines remain a strong force in the African American press. One of the most popular is *Ebony*, with a circulation of more than 1.3 million in 2017. Its mission

Black Entertainment Television

In 1980, the first television network made for African Americans was created. It was the brainchild of black entrepreneur Robert L. Johnson. After working in the cable industry, he saw that there was no real attempt to market television to African Americans. They were largely forgotten by the various networks of the time. As a result, Johnson started his own network: Black Entertainment Television (BET).

In the beginning, BET struggled to be profitable. Johnson had difficulty convincing advertisers that they should run ads on a network targeting African Americans. Eventually, however, BET surged in popularity. By 1991, it was the first black-controlled company traded on the New York Stock Exchange. Johnson sold it to Viacom in 2001 for the sum of $3 billion. This made Johnson the first African American billionaire. He used part of his proceeds to buy the Charlotte Bobcats, a professional basketball team, making him the first African American to own a major-league sports franchise.

Johnson remained CEO of BET under Viacom for a time, before stepping down in 2006. But the network continued on without him and remains popular. As of 2017, eighty-six million households in America have access to BET, making it the thirty-seventh most popular network in the country.

statement outlines its purpose: "*Ebony* is the No. 1 source for an authoritative perspective on the African American community. *Ebony* reflects the cross section of Black America as delivered by our best thinkers, our trendsetters, our activists, celebrities and next generation leaders. *Ebony* ignites conversation, promotes empowerment and celebrates aspiration. We are the heart, soul and pulse of Black America and a catalyst for reflection and progression." In addition to having a large number of readers, *Ebony* can boast that countless influential people have told their stories in its pages, including President Barack Obama.

The African American press has also been a part of the expansion of news sites on the internet. Like everyone today, African Americans now regularly receive news from online sources through their computers or phones, rather than from print sources. Many websites exist that write content for an African American audience. One popular site is *The Root,* which was launched in 2008. As of December 10, 2017, it was the 987th most popular website in the United States.

A Black Lives Matter protest in New York City on July 7, 2016

Black Lives Matter

Today, the African American press remains involved in fighting injustice. However, its leading role has perhaps been weakened in recent years. Filling the gap is one of the most prominent movements to stand up for African Americans in recent years: Black Lives Matter. Unlike the civil rights movements of the past, which were led by newspapers, organizations, or individual leaders, Black Lives Matter was created on social media. In 2013, the phrase was first written on Facebook by Patrisse Cullors in the wake of the murder acquittal of George Zimmerman—a neighborhood watch member—in the shooting death of an unarmed black teenager named Trayvon Martin. The hashtag took off on Twitter and soon became a national movement to end violence against African Americans, notably in the form of killings by police.

In this way, it was ordinary citizens on social media who promoted and made up Black Lives Matter. The African American press was not as closely involved in its beginnings as they often were in previous social justice movements. This waning influence of the press with the rise of social media is in no way restricted to the African American press—it is common in the mainstream press as well.

Many credit Black Twitter with the rise of the Black Lives Matter movement. According to journalist Jenna Wortham, "Black Twitter, as some call it, is not an actual place walled off from the rest of social media and is not a monolith; rather, it's a constellation of loosely formed multifaceted communities created spontaneously by and for black Twitter users who follow or promote black culture." These virtual communities often work together to fight injustice and promote a greater respect for human rights.

Just as in the past, when people like Frederick Douglass fought for women's rights, Black Lives Matter is also fighting for the rights of other marginalized groups. In 2014, one of the cofounders of the movement wrote a piece in *Ebony* that urged the movement to actively include black transgender people in its focus.

Many articles by members of Black Lives Matter have been published in other newspapers and magazines of the African American press. Pieces published in long-standing fixtures like the *Chicago Defender* have come to the movement's defense and urged readers to support it. In this way, the African American press remains heavily involved in the fight against injustice, even if social media is changing the press's role.

A Voice for Justice

From its beginning in 1827 to the present day, the African American press has been a champion of justice and equality. Never content to accept injustice, it first fought slavery and then Jim Crow and discrimination. Most recently, it has turned its attention to more insidious forms of racial injustice, such as police killings and voter ID laws that disenfranchise minorities.

Furthermore, the African American press has always supported the struggle of other oppressed groups. Its aims have never been insular. From its earliest days, prominent black abolitionists joined the fight of women.

Awards and Recognitions

For many years, the contributions of African American journalists were largely ignored and forgotten. Influential founders, editors, and contributors to African American publications did not receive mainstream awards for their work. Often, what attention they did receive focused on their attainments outside of print. For instance, A. Philip Randolph received the Presidential Medal of Freedom for his work as a "trade unionist and citizen"—his controversial publication the *Messenger* was not mentioned.

In recent years, this has changed. African American journalists are recognized more and more frequently for their contributions. As in the past, they often still use their voices to fight against injustice and try to benefit the marginalized of American society.

One such journalist who was recently honored is Cynthia Tucker. In 2007, she received the Pulitzer Prize for Commentary "for her courageous, clear-headed columns that evince a strong sense of morality and persuasive knowledge of the community." Some of the articles the award cited, written for the *Atlanta Journal-Constitution*, covered the issue of voter ID laws.

Many people consider these voter ID laws a thinly veiled attempt to disenfranchise minority voters. Tucker herself argued that Georgia's attempt to pass such a law "might have kept as many as 300,000 law-abiding citizens from voting, simply because they don't have driver's licenses. Many elderly and impoverished voters in rural areas of the state don't drive … But they are nevertheless regular voters." African American journalists like Cynthia Tucker remain a vocal force for justice in the United States.

Cynthia Tucker celebrates after learning she won the Pulitzer Prize.

They knew that the struggle for voting rights was not just the concern of African Americans but also of women and other groups that were discriminated against. Today, this concern with the rights of others is still strong. Black publications publish in support of Black Lives Matter, focusing not just on African Americans but also on the rights of transgender people and white victims of police violence as well.

This long history of constant struggle has led to amazing successes. The civil rights movement was aided greatly by the black press. It lent its pages to help organize the movement and fight the powerful institutions that oppressed black people around the country. It also led the way by speaking out against racism and discrimination for more than a century before the civil rights movement even began.

Throughout its storied history, the African American press has changed in many ways. Newspapers have declined in recent years—and the pamphlet format of early American history has virtually gone extinct. But today the black press has moved into television and the internet. Websites that reflect black voices have spread rapidly. Social media websites like Twitter have huge communities of black users who come together and share stories that affect them. The rise of social media seems poised to change not only the African American press but also the press and world in general.

What exactly the future will look like is uncertain. But what is sure is that African American journalists will continue to fight against injustice wherever it is found.

Chronology

1619 The first enslaved Africans arrive in colonial British North America at Jamestown, Virginia.

1776 The United States declares its independence from Great Britain. Despite the misgivings of some Founding Fathers, slavery is allowed to continue in the new nation.

1827 *Freedom's Journal*, the first newspaper owned and operated by African Americans, is founded in New York City.

1829 African American David Walker publishes the pamphlet *Walker's Appeal*, which denounces slavery in the United States.

1848 The first women's rights convention in America is held at Seneca Falls. Black abolitionist Frederick Douglass attends and supports the movement in his newspaper, the *North Star*.

1859 White abolitionist John Brown leads his ill-fated raid on the federal arsenal at Harpers Ferry. Black newspapers—and later Northern white newspapers— celebrate his daring action, while he is demonized in the South.

1865 The Thirteenth Amendment, outlawing slavery except as punishment for a crime, is ratified.

1916 Spurred by the *Chicago Defender*, the Great Migration begins as black people living in the rural South move in large numbers to Northern cities.

1919 The Red Summer breaks out across the United States as race riots and lynchings result in hundreds of deaths.

1931 In Scottsboro, Alabama, nine African Americans are arrested after a white woman is coerced by police to accuse them of rape. The trial of the Scottsboro Boys is covered extensively by the black press.

1942 During World War II, the *Pittsburgh Courier* begins its Double V for Victory campaign to defeat America's enemies abroad and racism at home.

1955 Fourteen-year-old Emmett Till is lynched in Mississippi. Pictures of his body at an open-casket funeral galvanize the civil rights movement.

1968 Martin Luther King Jr. is assassinated; the civil rights movement comes to an end as the last of a flurry of laws protecting the rights of African Americans is passed.

1980 BET (Black Entertainment Television) is founded. It is the first TV channel that caters specifically to an African American audience.

2013 The Black Lives Matter movement begins in the United States.

Glossary

abject Hopeless or miserable.

abolitionists People who opposed slavery and sought to bring about its end—or abolition.

anathemas Curses or extreme denunciations.

approbation Approval.

catalyst Something that brings about a change.

civil rights movement A historical movement for greater protection under the law for African Americans. It is typically dated from 1954 to 1968 and was spearheaded by leaders like Martin Luther King Jr.

disenfranchisement Being deprived of the right to vote.

expediency Suitability or usefulness.

exude To ooze or draw out.

fascism A dictatorial form of government where opposition is not tolerated. World War II was often characterized as a war on fascism due to the Nazi government of Germany and fascist Italy.

franchise The right to vote.

indolent Lazy.

Jim Crow The legal system of racial segregation and discrimination that held sway in the South for nearly a century after the end of slavery.

Liberia An African country that was promoted as a home for former American slaves. Various groups helped finance the return of freedmen to the country and supported its independence and a government modeled on that of the United States.

man-of-war A warship of the era.

manumission The freeing of one's slaves.

McCarthy era A historical period in the 1950s when Senator Joseph McCarthy led a high-profile witch-hunt to root out alleged communists.

monolith A single, large block of stone. It is often metaphorically used to refer to something that is unified or uniform.

NAACP The National Association for the Advancement of Colored People; founded in 1909, the NAACP played a key role in many important events in African American history.

promulgate To publish or proclaim.

Reconstruction Era The historical period lasting from the end of the Civil War in 1865 to 1877. The federal government attempted to promote racial equality in the South, but efforts failed. When federal soldiers departed the South in 1877, a system of racial segregation developed.

Red Summer The summer of 1919; many race riots and lynchings occurred throughout the United States as racial tensions boiled over.

UNIA The Universal Negro Improvement and Conservation Association and African Communities League; founded by Marcus Garvey, UNIA was a massive social movement among African Americans during the early 1920s.

yellow journalism The use of sensationalist stories to make money. The term also refers to the historical era of journalism when this became widespread—the turn of the twentieth century.

Further Information

Books

Elliot, Henry. *Frederick Douglass: From Slavery to Statesman.* New York: Crabtree Publishing Company, 2009.

Michaeli, Ethan. *The Defender: How the Legendary Black Newspaper Changed America.* New York: Houghton Mifflin Harcourt, 2016.

Senna, Carl. *The Black Press and the Struggle for Civil Rights.* Danbury, CT: Scholastic Library Publishing, 1994.

Websites

The Black Press: Soldiers Without Swords
http://www.pbs.org/blackpress/film/index.html

Find photos, a timeline, and a full transcript of PBS's documentary about the history of the African American press.

History of the *Chicago Defender*
https://chicagodefender.com/about/history-of-the-chicago-defender

The *Chicago Defender* outlines its own history and accomplishments.

Jim Crow Laws and Racial Segregation
https://socialwelfare.library.vcu.edu/eras/civil-war-reconstruction/jim-crow-laws-andracial-segregation

Virginia Commonwealth University explains the history of Jim Crow and segregation in the United States.

Slavery in America
http://www.history.com/topics/black-history/slavery

History.com gives a brief overview of slavery in the United States along with a video on the topic.

Videos
Civil Rights Movement
http://www.history.com/topics/black-history/civil-rights-movement/videos

View many short videos about the civil rights movement.

"Why African Americans Left the South in Droves—And What's Bringing Them Back"
https://www.youtube.com/watch?v=VCdTyl141bA

Vox presents the history of the Great Migration and the recent trend toward its reversal.

Bibliography

Bacon, Jacqueline. "The History of Freedom's Journal: A
    Study in Empowerment and Community." *Journal of
    African American History* 88, no. 1 (2003): 1–20.

Blakemore, Erin. "This African-American Artist's Cartoons
    Helped Win World War II." Smithsonian.com, February
    27, 2017. https://www.smithsonianmag.com/smart-
    news/african-american-artists-cartoons-helped-win-
    world-war-ii-180962279.

Carter, Dan T. *Scottsboro: A Tragedy of the American South.*
    Baton Rouge: Louisiana State University Press, 2007.

Douglass, Frederick. *Narrative of the Life of Frederick
    Douglass.* Mineola, NY: Dover Publications, 1995.

Du Bois, Willian Edward Burghardt. "Editorial." *Crisis: A
    Record of the Darker Races* (New York), November 1910.

"Ghastly Deeds of Race Rioters Told." *Chicago Defender*
    (Chicago), August 2, 1919.

Goings, Kenneth W. "Memphis Free Speech." *The Tennessee Encyclopedia of History and Culture*, February 21, 2011. http://tennesseeencyclopedia.net/entry.php?rec=894.

González, Juan, and Joseph Torres. *News for All People: The Epic Story of Race and the American Media.* New York: Verso, 2012.

Johnson, Robert, and Brian Dumaine. "The Market Nobody Wanted." CNN, October 1, 2002. http://money.cnn.com/magazines/fsb/fsb_archive/2002/10/01/330571/index.htm.

Kusmer, Kenneth L., and Joe W. Trotter, eds. *African American Urban History Since World War II.* Chicago: University of Chicago Press, 2009.

Lennig, Arthur. "Myth and Fact: The Reception of 'The Birth of a Nation.'" *Film History* 16, no. 2 (2004): 117–141.

Simmons, Charles A. *The African American Press: A History of News Coverage During National Crises, with Special Reference to Four Black Newspapers, 1827–1965.* Jefferson, NC: McFarland, 2006.

"They Glory in Their Shame." *Colored American* (New York), June 10, 1837. http://nationalhumanitiescenter.org/pds/maai/community/text6/coloredamerican.pdf.

Washburn, Patrick S. *The African American Newspaper: Voice of Freedom.* Evanston, IL: Northwestern University Press, 2006.

Wilkerson, Isabel. "The Long-Lasting Legacy of the Great Migration." Smithsonian.com, September 2016. https://www.smithsonianmag.com/history/long-lasting-legacy-great-migration-180960118.

Index

About the Author

Derek Miller is a writer and educator from Salisbury, Maryland. He is the author of several books, including *Focus on Africa: The Economy in Contemporary Africa* and *Fighting for Their Country: Minority Soldiers Fighting in World War I*. When he is not writing, teaching, or researching topics in science and history, Derek enjoys traveling with his wife.